Seashells Brought In From The Ocean

Salamah E. Farooque

BookLeaf Publishing
India | USA | UK

Presentation by *BookLeaf Publishing*

Web: www.bookleafpub.com

E-mail: info@bookleafpub.com

ISBN: 9789357215534

First edition 2022

To my family,

For always having my back.

Mind Reading

As a child the world resides on surface level
appearances,
People's expressions their body language, their
words,
You viewed things based on what was given to
you:
A smile showed happiness,
A frown implied wrath and anger,
Tears were the mark of sadness,
Soft words reassurance,
Eventually, things change.
"I'm fine," is no longer assurance that all is well,
A smile does not guarantee amity,
Hidden agendas lurk in every corner,
Implications and questions begin to arise.
"I wonder what she's thinking,"
"Did he mean what he said?"
"I bet they hate me,"
"Oh no, I probably made a fool of myself,"
Around, around these thoughts travel,
As if chasing one another but never being
caught.
Guesses are made,
Doubts are shaped,
Assumptions reign,

Heartbreak follows,
Fights explode,
Sleep evades,
As you wonder and wonder,
What travels through another's mind,
Wishing dearly you could take a peek,
Only to realise,
That your thoughts may be mirrored,
And you were never the first,
To have the desire to mind read another.

Life In The Pages

The gift wrapper comes off as light attacks,
Across your face a smile cracks,
You stroke the navy of my front cover,
Rifling through the pages within, your fingers
hover.

Musing, you have your pen in your grip,
Tapping your writing tool against your lip,
Sunlight filters through your window,
Casting the edges of your body in a halo.

The words come easily now,
Especially when you get into rows,
In the dark and lonely corner of your bed,
Ink jabs into my flesh as you empty out your
head.

Initially, I hated the pain,
Until I saw how your heart was slain
Wetness dropped like bombs onto me,
I flew into the wall as you sobbed tearily.

One day you reached the last page,
Your face crumpled almost in rage,
You sighed and drew me to a close,

Before you put me on a shelf to pose.

I eventually shift things around my room,
Eyeing my navy book of gloom,
A shiver passes through me, and I choose,
To put it under my bed next to the shoes.

Through sun, rain, wind, and snow
I marvel as I see myself grow,
Later I decide to approve,
That it's the right time to move.

I finally enter to fulfil my chore,
Packing up my room is such a bore,
I absently fill boxes which will be taken to the
van,
Beneath my bed, something detracts me from
my original plan.

I don't recognise the navy journal,
Sitting down, I journey into my past internal,
Hours pass and light dims to black outside,
I finally turn the last page of my teenage mind.

I wipe my cheeks that are damp,
How could they not be? when heady feelings
clamp
My adult heart which can only be awed
At what my prior self endured.

Mixed Race, Biracial, Etc.

There's one side
And another
White
Brown
Forks, knives, spoons
Bread and hands
French
Urdu
Bland food
Spiced dishes
Western clothes
Shalwar kameez
Rain and cold
Sun and heat
Sunburnt
Tanned
Blunt speech
Hospitable smiles
Europe
Asia
Individuality
Community
Secular
Islamic State

Coloniser
Colonised
Mont Blanc
K2
French revolution
Partition

And then there's me:
Racially ambiguous
Culturally conflicted
Bilingual
French not Urdu
Looks more Asian less European
A marvel
An oddity
Belonging to both
Belonging to neither
Not fitting in a box
Yet loving my uniqueness
At war with myself
At peace with myself
Questioning who I am
Enrichened by experiences
Opportunity to discover
Opportunity to appreciate
Opportunity to accept
Opportunity to be
Me

Personal Space

Mum, Don't go through
my stuff. There's things
I don't want you
to see. Please. Respect
my request. I'm not
being mean. Just don't
want to be seen
as anything different. Imagine
this is your mind;
you would not want
me crawling through it.

Hazy Fairy Tale

Wind heavy with heat,
Waving through my hair,
Morning sun beats down on my arms,
Go to the kitchen when breakfast is called,
Take my paratha and omelette back outside,
Sit on the woven bench in the courtyard,
Dig in with relish,
Lick my fingers when I'm done.

Later to stave off the heat,
Dash between clothing lines with my water gun,
As I spray my siblings,
Shrieking with glee.

For dinner we go to my aunt's house,
Cross the perilous road which divides us,
Greet my cousins, aunt, uncle when we arrive,
Sit around talking, laughing,
Play badminton in the entryway courtyard,
Among the plants, dim space lit by stark
lighting,
Come to the dinner table to eat,
Return home late,
Belly full, heart fulfilled.

Packing Up

Packing up everything is the task at hand,
It is more than that however,
The hallway is a memory lane,
Photographs hung up displaying captured
moments,
Your bedroom was always a cosy spot,
A place of comfort, sleep, and relaxation,
The smell of various meals clings to the kitchen
walls,
Where you have cooked, tasted, burned,
Many a sauna session took place in the
bathroom,
As warm water soothed your tired muscles,
The living room was a guaranteed place of
entertainment,
Host to every party, movie marathon and gaming
session.

Boxes fill up all spaces in this small apartment,
It's one room really,
This is where my living room, bedroom and
kitchen will be,
All moments compressed into one,
The walls crowd in on me,
I want to go back.

Period, Sis

Red is the colour of shame.
Disgusting,
ugly,
unwanted.
Forget it
if it feels like your insides are constantly
demanding attention by causing you pain.
Like an intense stomach-ache
mingled with aches all over.
Tensed up
failing to relax.
Menstruation not only cripples you,
messes up plans,
plays with your moods:
taboo still surrounds periods.
No excuse,
come to work,
don't discuss it.
God forbid you make anyone feel
uncomfortable.
Let's also remember that sanitary products
are taxed since they're luxury items.
Never knew that the blood flowing out of me
was preventable, an option I chose.
And, yes,

it is also something to be mocked:
Why so emotional?
Wait, are you on your period?
No wonder you're so bipolar.
Funny how some of us can stand
poker faced while experiencing stabbing cramps.
At least between us women
we can vent,
laugh,
support.
Hey, you got a spare pad?
Sure thing, here you go.
When that first day hits
or second or third
or however many.
The considerate ones
will willingly buy you your products,
medicine,
chocolate.
Accidently burn themselves as they pour boiling
water
in a hot water bottle.
Prepare your favourite hot beverage.
Tell you to rest up,
keep watching,
napping,
distracting,
as they get on with errands
you were meant to do.

It's not always easy
but it's worth the effort.
It's a natural bodily process,
so enough with the shaming,
unsolicited jokes,
ignorance.
It's about time that things changed.

Hearing Aids On Or Off?

Clocks make a ticking sound,
I can only hear it with my hearing aids on.

Everyone complains about the noisy pub down
the road,
Well, I can't hear it and fall asleep immediately.

There's a weird sound like a rustling hum when I
have them on,
Oh, wait, it's just still air.

Is it better to have headphones to put over the
aids?
Or earphones where I have to take them out?

Whoops, don't go with them in the shower,
They'll get damaged I know that.

Swimming is a tricky one,
Encourage shouting, that'll help make up the
difference.

Ugh, they're all the way upstairs,
Can I really be bothered to get them?
Oh well, I'll settle for subtitles on the TV…

…Or really loud volume if no one's home.

Ah, long days on end at home,
My ears can rest from the noisiness brought on
by the aids,
No pressure on my ear canal,
Goodbye earaches until next time.

Wait…where'd they go?
I need them for school tomorrow!
Never shall I leave them lying around,
I vow for the millionth time.

I forgot to pack hearing aid batteries,
And they're out of juice,
Just when I go up to my interviewer,
Who doesn't see my aids behind my headscarf.

Time for a convoluted explanation,
For why she has to shout her questions
Unless she wants to repeat herself,
Three or four or ten times.

Purrfect Life

Sleeping where the warm light hits me,
On something soft,
Like what those tall creatures sleep on at night,
Or sit on to stare at moving pictures.

Observing everything from a high place,
As tall creatures walk down below,
And winged beings move through the air,
Return to my warm abode when I am done.

Salivate at that gorgeous smell,
Miaowing to get my tall creature's attention,
Chew on soft, delicious flesh,
Lick my chops when I am full.

Prepare to clean every inch of myself,
Crane my neck to lick my back,
Wet my paws to scrub behind my ears,
Bite my claws to get rid of dirt.

Protect my territory when I see an intruder,
My hair rises high as my tail puffs up,
I spit and hiss harshly,
Sit proudly when the other being like me runs
off.

Tumultuous Interior

torn heart, cleaved in two
shocked limbs unable to move
mind removed from all

like water ripples
numbness spreads through my body
nothing matters now

WaRm RaYs Of SuNsHiNe
CaReSs My BoNeS lIkE bLaNkEtS
rAiNbOwS fIlL tHe WoRlD

sKiPpInG gIdDiLy
EnDoPhInS pOp LiKe BuBbLeS
lAuGhTeR sPiLlS oVeR

HOT BOILING LAVA
CORROSIVE TASTE CHARS MY HEART
DRAGON EXPELS FIRE

DESTRUCTIVE SHAKING
KETTLE CAN'T CONTAIN WATER
IT SPEWS OUT, I PUNCH

Rules Of Work

1. Smile to appear approachable
2. Avoid sighing when a bad song comes up
3. Pass the time chatting with colleagues
4. Assess if a customer is in a bad mood
5. Ignore sarcastic comments from rude customers
6. Walk through the shop floor to prevent feet cramps
7. Eat a lot during your break
8. Carry painkillers in case of a headache
9. Don't look at the time too often
10. Be careful cutting cardboard boxes
11. Run after customers who left their wallets at the till
12. Engage in conversations with chatty customers
13. Trudge out of the shop en route home

Lovable Annoyances

You're never alone
Which can be a pain
They're always around
Screaming, laughing, crying
It's like, can I get some quiet?
Careful what you wish for
There are tangled limbs
Full on fights
Shout
Argue
Ceasefire
Shy
Reconcile
Can't you ever get your own snack
No, share it, you're not the only one
Eat full speed
Like rabid animals
Stolen food
Didn't you put a label?
Even then it's not full-proof
Stolen clothes
Hand me downs
Power dynamics:
Oldest
Middle

Youngest
Age doesn't matter though
You realise this the more you grow
Despite how absurd it seems
That a baby might one day
Get on with a decade older person
You're practically from different generations
Who cares
You'll end up learning or teaching
Life advice comes from the home
Hold onto it
It'll be your lifeline when you separate
Celebrate each other's success
No longer need to snitch or fight
Recognising each other's worth
Means respecting each person as an individual
Tell that to younger you
You would have laughed and called you crazy:
There's no way we'd ever get on
She scratched, I bit, he poked, I snarled
I wanted peace not them.
Well, the house is silent now
They've all left, you're last
No rivals
No confiders
No noise
You got what you wanted
Right?

A Single Drop

A single drop,
Bursting through the soil,
Alone it is powerless to move,
Come clones and change begins to happen,
A small puddle,
A thin trickle,
Building in power it becomes a stream,
Weaving its way downhill,
Through blades of green,
Cutting them down to form a bed,
Upon which it can slide smoothly.

Obstacles in its path do not stop it,
Wind its way around rocks,
A translucent snake moving through the land,
Pretty soon organisms inhabit it,
Fish matching the speed of the rushing river,
Water striders gliding along the surface,
Reeds poking up into the air.

Bigger and bigger it grows,
So deep it is impossible to wade across,
Then one day the river meets a rival,
It is not linear, nor full of twists,
This new force takes up all available space,

Expansive, with no end in sight,
Journeying through land is at an end,
The sea claims its new source of replenishment.

The Perfect Canvas

Rice—
The perfect canvas,
Upon it many dishes can merge;
Korma, Daal, Biryani,
Splashes of sauce,
Sprinkles of spices,
Transform the look—
Knolls of lamb,
Rising above the coloured white,
Pebbles of lentil,
Litter the former snow,
Shrubs of parsley,
Peek between pigmented daisy petals.
The unity of ingredients and smells,
Extends beyond the meal itself,
It is hard to judge,
How many portions are needed,
Extras invite more than one,
To feast at the table,
Chatter infuses the air above the food,
Warmth does not come from the dishes alone,
It fills the heart as well as the stomach.
A blank canvas,
Exists to become something greater.

Travel Necessities

To pack:
-Clothes
-Toiletries
-Charger
-Sunglasses
-Sunscreen
-A cap
-A traveller's mindset

Remember
-Don't lose your passport
-Or your money
-Be adventurous
-Try new things
-Meet people
-Go sightseeing
-Relax
-Be yourself
-Drink water

Bring back:
-Souvenirs
-Memories
-Experience
-Photos

-A satisfied heart
-Self-growth
-A smile
-A tan
-Dirty laundry
-A refreshed mindset

It Was Just A Joke

It was just a joke
Relax
Why so serious?
Take a chill pill
It's not that deep.

It was just a joke
Sticks and stones
Not like you're physically hurt
Toughen up
You're so sensitive.

It was just a joke
I'm lying in bed
Dreading tomorrow
Tears fall to my ears
As harmless, heavy words bludgeon my skull.

It was just a joke
Everyone's looking at me
I'm sure they're all judging
I'm so pathetic
I can't speak up
Who will listen?

It was just a jok—
"No, it's not, apologise,"
I look up in shock
The bullies are dumbfounded
My classmate turns to me
"Tell me if they ever say mean things again
Words hurt as much as blows
They get into your head
Make you feel all alone."

It was not a joke
I thought I was delusional
I didn't understand why I cared so much
I tried to ignore it all
But my feelings shouldn't be dismissed
I know that now.

Wonderments And Weirdness

The mind processes events of the day,
Subconscious surfaces, is what they say,
Buried memories light up behind your eyes
The lowest lows and the highest highs.

Strangers inhabit your dreamland,
No, you've seen them before,
But like sand slipping from your hand,
Recollection fades into nothing more.

You're in a heightened reality,
Without the rules of society,
Teleportation, for instance, is a norm,
Find yourself travelling from a glacier to a dorm.

Shut-eye time makes your mind excitable,
You take your environment as fact,
Not questioning it makes you gullible,
But rationality is possible for those with tact.

Choose where you go,
Break the flow,
Make your own choices,
Retain your voice,

In the land of wonderments and weirdness.

I Wish

How is his house so aesthetic?
Comment: cute, heart emoji,
They're such relationship goals,
Double tap,
Gosh, I want a body like hers,
Comment: You're so gorgeous!
I wish I could have their lives,
I look around me:
Cramped studio flat,
Thumbs down,
Only other being a cat,
#lonelyandsingle #sadlife,
Empty pizza boxes and fizzy drink cans,
Comment: getting fat.

Post a picture of wifey and me,
We were making lunch together,
She got an urgent call and left,
I had to finish our meal alone,
One month later,
I file for divorce,
I wish she had treated me better.

Post my house tour video,
Sigh as I turn back to my paperwork,

I wish I could spend more time at home,
What's the point of a nice house I don't live in?
I'm too tired to appreciate it when I'm there,
Maybe I should downsize,
So I don't have to work as hard.

Post my summer outfits compilation,
Take a sip of my lemon juice,
Scrunch up my nose at the sour taste,
I wish sweets were healthy,
I'm going to the gym,
Can't miss cardio,
Hope I don't faint like last time,
My doctor said I'm dangerously slim,
She doesn't get it though,
Everyone tells me I'm beautiful like this.

Franglais

I find it fascinant,
[I find it fascinating,]
Que je peux read these mots,
[That I can read these words,]
Without breaking mon rythme,
[Without breaking my flow,]
Thanks to le pouvoir du bilinguisme,
[Thanks to the power of bilingualism,]
Qui me permet de switch between,
[Which allows me to switch between,]
More than une langue,
[More than one language,]
Comme si j'avais a superpower,
[As if I had a superpower,]
Which resides dans les mots that I know,
[Which resides in the words that I know,]
Creating une langue hybride,
[Creating a hybrid language,]
That is not recorded dans les textbooks,
[That is not recorded in textbooks,]
Mais qui est still legitimate,
[But which is still legitimate,]
Since other dual language parlants,
[Since other dual language speakers,]
Vont avoir a similar way of communicating,

[Will have a similar way of communicating,]
And will comprendrent ce que tu dis,
[And will understand what you say,]
It works to fill in les blancs,
[It works to fill in the blanks,]
Pour les words que tu oublies,
[For the words that you forget,]
In one language and pick up dans l'autre,
[In one language and pick up in the other,]
C'est comme une dance,
[It's like a dance,]
Merging la grammaire et le vocabulaire,
[Merging grammar and vocabulary,]
Qui viennent de deux different cultures,
[Which come from two different cultures,]
Which helps continuer une conversation sans
pause,
[Which helps to continue a conversation without
a break,]
C'est messy et unpredictable,
[It's messy and unpredictable,]
Ce qui rend this non-existent langue,
[Which makes this non-existent language,]
Beautiful et charmant.
[Beautiful and appealing.]

Wordless

White
Is the colour of a blank page,
Hopeful
Words can fill up the space,
Despairing
No ideas come forth,
Bored
Fingers fiddle with the pen,
Scour
The entire expanse of the mind,
Fruitless
Return to aimless staring,
Walk
Get those neurons sparking,
Slump
It is pointless,
Dig
Nails into scalp,
Scribble
Get the creativity stimulated,
Sigh
Might as well leave it,
Blink
Maybe something has changed,
Focus

The mind is ruminating,
Interruption
The spark is extinguished,
Stand
Leave the desk,
Return
Days later,
Resume
This mental standstill.

Freedom

Freedom tastes like air cutting your throat,
Breathless as you inhale wintry, mountainous
atmosphere,
Standing at the top of that peak,
Vertiginous, on top of the world.

Freedom smells like freshly cut grass,
Or morning frost turned to dew,
Sweet sounding like the call of birds,
As they take flight,
Feeling the wind ruffling their feathers,
Knowing they are untouchable to everyone
below,
No shackles holding them to the ground.

Freedom looks like light at the end of a tunnel,
Assurance that you can sigh with relief,
Gaze upon the smile of loved ones,
At liberty to know that they are fine.

Freedom is a boulder coming off your chest,
The allowance to embrace without limit,
Motor rumbling steadily beneath your feet,
As you drive full speed toward the dipping sun,
Shouting at the top of your lungs,

Just because you can.

Freedom in any form, shape, or size,
Must be experienced,
To feel alive.